# COLOUR the ZODIAC

igloobooks

igloobooks

Published in 2021
First published in the UK by Igloo Books Ltd
An imprint of Igloo Books Ltd
Cottage Farm, NN6 0BJ, UK
Owned by Bonnier Books
Sveavägen 56, Stockholm, Sweden
www.igloobooks.com



0821 001
2 4 6 8 10 9 7 5 3 1
ISBN 978-1-80108-353-9

Designed by Simon Parker
Edited by Hannah Cather

Printed and manufactured in China

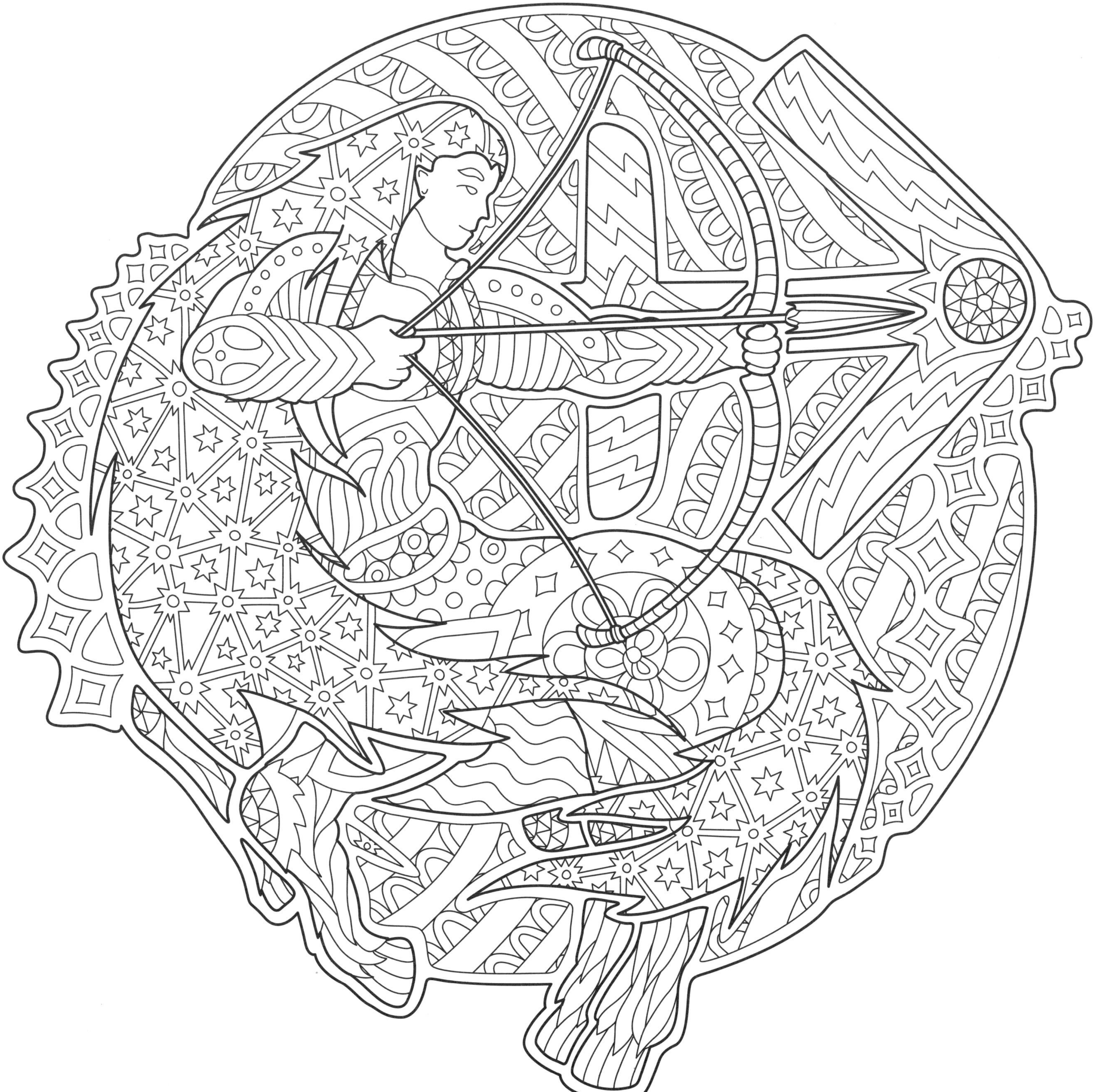

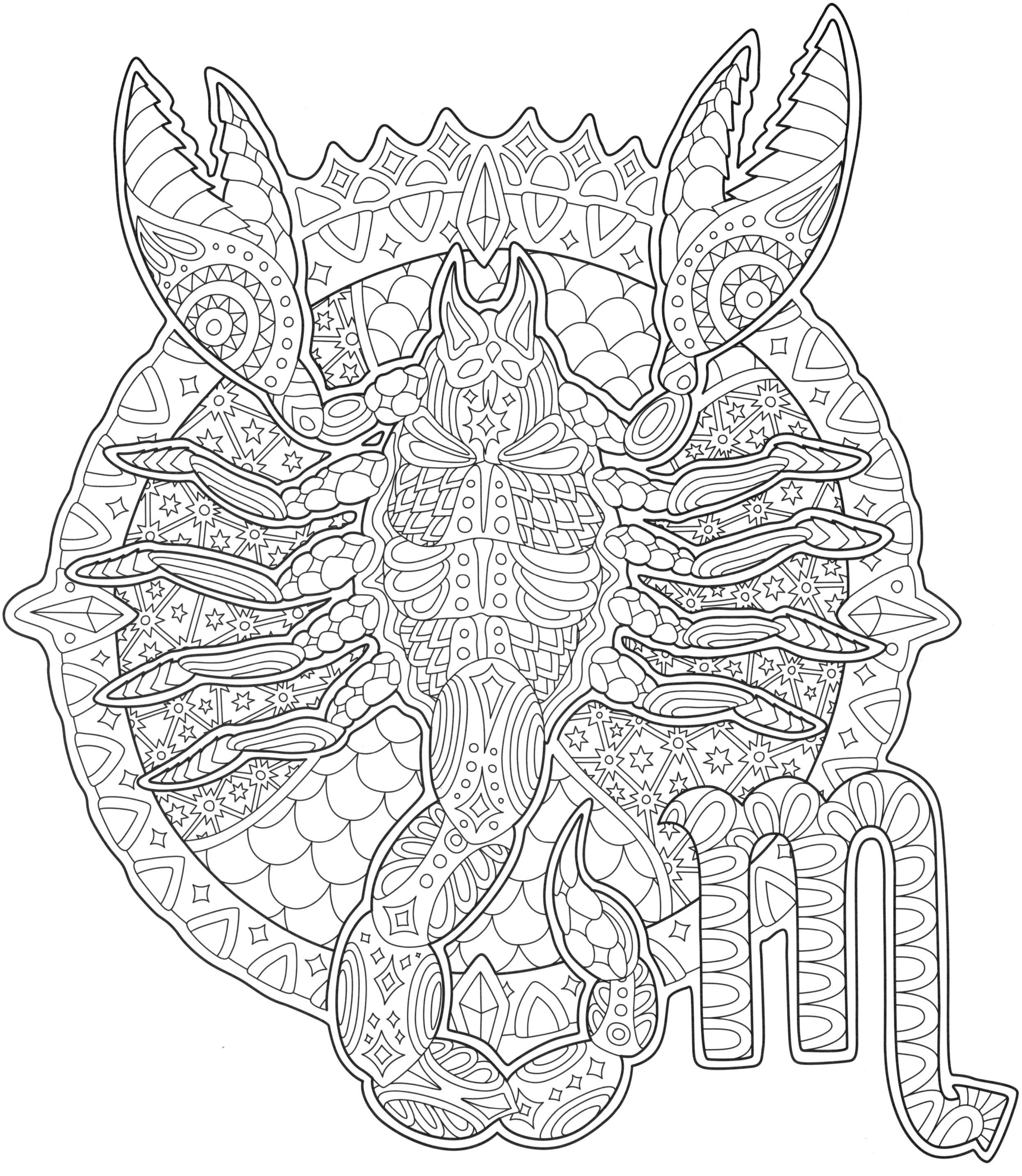